W9-BBF-558

# WARSHIPS

by Jeffrey Zuehlke

Lerner Publications Company • Minneapolis

*For Graham*

Text copyright © 2006 by Lerner Publications Company

All rights reserved. International copyright secured. No part of this book may be reproduced, stored in a retrieval system, or transmitted in any form or by any means—electronic, mechanical, photocopying, recording, or otherwise—without the prior written permission of Lerner Publications Company, except for the inclusion of brief quotations in an acknowledged review.

Lerner Publications Company
A division of Lerner Publishing Group
241 First Avenue North
Minneapolis, MN 55401 U.S.A.

Website address: www.lernerbooks.com

Words in **bold type** are explained in a glossary on page 30.

Library of Congress Cataloging-in-Publication Data

Zuehlke, Jeffrey, 1968–
    Warships / by Jeffrey Zuehlke.
       p.   cm. – (Pull ahead books)
    Includes index.
    ISBN–13: 978–8225–2866–1 (lib. bdg. : alk. paper)
    ISBN–10: 0–8225–2866–5 (lib. bdg. : alk. paper)
    1. Warships—United States—Juvenile literature. I. Title.
II. Series.
VA58.4.Z84 2006
623.825'0973–dc22              2005001207

Manufactured in the United States of America
1-32588-3622-6/22/2016

Look out on
the water!
What kind of
ship is this?

It is a warship. Warships sail all around the world.

Warships are built to fight. This warship is part of the U.S. Navy. The U.S. Navy has many kinds of warships.

This is an **aircraft carrier**. Aircraft carriers are the biggest warships.

Aircraft carriers are like airports on the water. Airplanes can take off and land on them.

This warship is called a **cruiser**. Cruisers are smaller than aircraft carriers.

Cruisers carry many weapons. This cruiser is firing a **missile**.

This warship is a **destroyer**.
Destroyers protect aircraft carriers.
They have many missiles and guns.

Destroyers and other warships sail
in groups.

Who is in charge of a warship?
The captain!

The captain is in charge of the sailors on a warship. Sailors keep the warship running. Every sailor has an important job.

These sailors
are loading a
gun on a
warship.

# This sailor is looking for other warships.

This sailor is working on a warship's engine. Warships have huge engines.

How does a warship move?  Engines
turn a warship's **propellers**.  Spinning
propellers push a warship through
the water.

Warship propellers are huge. They are on the bottom of a warship.

The bottom of a warship is called its **hull**. The hull is the main part of a warship.

The top of the hull is called the deck.

The parts of a warship above the deck are called the **superstructure**.

The bridge is a room inside the superstructure. A sailor steers a warship from the bridge. Full speed ahead!

Warships spend many months at sea.
A warship's time at sea is called
its **deployment**.

This warship's deployment is over. It is sailing home.

These sailors have been away from home for a long time. They want to see their family and friends.

These people are excited to see their favorite sailors!

This sailor is happy to be home. He is saying hello to his new baby!

# Facts about Warships

■ Each U.S. Navy warship has a name. A warship's name starts with the letters "USS." "USS" stands for "United States ship."

■ The U.S. Navy names its cruisers after famous battles in the country's history. For example, the USS *Bunker Hill* is named after a famous battle of the American Revolution.

■ Destroyers in the U.S. Navy are named after famous people. The USS *John Paul Jones* is named after a famous sailor. Jones fought for the United States during the American Revolution.

■ Most of the aircraft carriers in the U.S. Navy are named after presidents of the country. The USS *George Washington* is named after the first president of the United States.

# Parts of a Warship

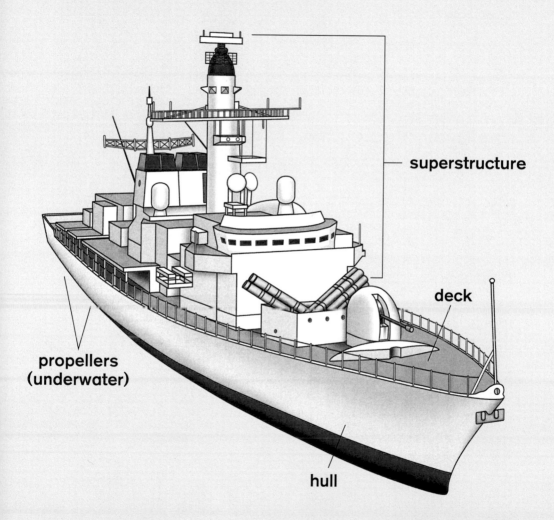

superstructure

deck

propellers
(underwater)

hull

# Glossary

**aircraft carrier:** a very large warship that can take airplanes all around the world

**cruiser:** a warship that carries many weapons

**deployment:** the period of time that a warship spends at sea and away from home

**destroyer:** a fast and powerful warship that protects aircraft carriers

**hull:** the main part of a warship

**missile:** a large weapon on a warship

**propellers:** parts of a warship that spin and push a warship through the water

**superstructure:** parts of a warship that rise above the deck

# Index

# About the Author

Jeffrey Zuehlke isn't much of a sailor, but he loves ships and reading about the U.S. Navy. He lives in Minneapolis, Minnesota, with his land-lubber family.

## Photo Acknowledgments

The photographs in this book appear courtesy of: U.S. Navy Photo, Front Cover, pp. 3, 4, 5, 6, 7, 8, 9, 10, 11, 12, 13, 14, 15, 16, 17, 18, 19, 20, 21, 22, 23, 24, 25, 26, 27, 31. Illustration on p. 29 by Laura Westlund, © Lerner Publications Company.